AMERICAN
HUMANE

Protecting Children & Animals Since 1877

Beginning Pet Care

WITH AMERICAN HUMANE

Learning to Care for a CAT

Bailey Books
an imprint of

Enslow Publishers, Inc.

40 Ind...
Box 3...
Berke...
USA

Felicia Lowenstein Niven

AMERICAN HUMANE

Protecting Children & Animals Since 1877

Founded in 1877, the American Humane Association is the only national organization dedicated to protecting both children and animals. Through a network of child and animal protection agencies and individuals, American Humane develops policies, legislation, curricula, and training programs — and takes action — to protect children and animals from abuse, neglect, and exploitation. To learn how you can support American Humane's vision of a nation where no child or animal will ever be a victim of abuse or neglect, visit www.americanhumane. org, phone (303) 792-9900, or write to the American Humane Association at 63 Inverness Drive East, Englewood, Colorado, 80112-5117.

To our Readers:

We have done our best to make sure all Internet Addresses in this book were active and appropriate when we went to press. However, the author and the publisher have no control over and assume no liability for the material available on those Internet sites or on other Web sites they may link to. Any comments or suggestions can be sent by e-mail to comments@enslow.com or to the address on the back cover.

Every effort has been made to locate all copyright holders of material used in this book. If any errors or omissions have occurred, corrections will be made in future editions of this book.

To my husband James, who introduced me to the joy of cats.

Bailey Books, an imprint of Enslow Publishers, Inc.

Copyright © 2011 by Enslow Publishers, Inc.

Library of Congress Cataloging-in-Publication Data

Niven, Felicia Lowenstein.
  Learning to care for a cat / Felicia Lowenstein Niven.
    p. cm. — (Beginning pet care with American Humane)
  Includes bibliographical references and index.
  Summary: "Readers will learn how to choose, train, and care for a cat"—Provided by publisher.
  ISBN 978-0-7660-3191-3
  1. Cats—Juvenile literature. I. Title.
  SF445.7.N58 2010
  636.8—dc22
                            2008048963

Printed in China

052010 Leo Paper Group, Heshan City, Guangdong, China

10 9 8 7 6 5 4 3 2 1

Illustration Credits: All animals in logo bar and boxes, Shutterstock. © The British Museum/ Topham/The Image Works, pp. 10–11; © istockphoto.com/Chris Rose, pp. 3 (thumbnail 6), 9, 44; © istockphoto.com/Steve Burger, pp. 3 (thumbnail 1), 5; Jupiterimages.com, pp. 3 (thumbnail 2), 13; Mark McQueen/KimballStock, pp. 1, 22–23; © Mary Kate Denny/PhotoEdit, p. 21; © Michael Newman/PhotoEdit, p. 42; © Myrleen Ferguson Cate/PhotoEdit, pp. 3 (thumbnail 4), 25; © Richard Hutchings/PhotoEdit, p. 35; © Richard Levine/Alamy, p. 18; Ron Kimball/KimballStock, p. 39; Shutterstock, pp. 3 (thumbnails 3, 5), 4, 6, 14, 15, 17, 24, 27, 28, 31, 32, 36, 41 © Thomas Michael Corcoran/PhotoEdit, p. 19.

Cover Illustration: Mark McQueen/KimballStock (cat on his back).

Table of Contents

Chapter 1

Rescue

The call came in on a chilly spring morning. A mother cat and her two kittens were in danger!

Peggy wrote down the details. She and her friends volunteer for LICK. That is short for Life Improvement for Cats and Kittens. It is a group that rescues cats and kittens and finds them good homes.

Rescue

Many groups around the United States rescue cats and kittens.

Peggy was worried. The cats were living in a garbage dumpster behind the local mall. It was cold and dirty. There was no food or water. LICK had to get there right away.

Colleen was the first to arrive. She carefully stepped over the smelly garbage. There they were! But the cats did not let Colleen get close.

Rescue groups take care of kittens and cats until they are ready to be adopted.

Colleen set out traps. The traps are wire mesh boxes with food inside. When the cat walks in, she steps on a ramp. That makes the door drop. Then she cannot escape. Sometimes the door scares the cat, but it does not hurt her.

6

Rescue

Rescuers never leave a trap alone. They need to make sure that the cat is okay. After the trap's door closes, a rescuer quickly covers the trap with a blanket. This helps the animal feel safe.

Colleen did not have long to wait. The food smelled so good. The cats were hungry. The mother cat and one kitten walked right in. But then something happened.

There was a loud clang. It was the sound of the door closing. It scared the other kitten. She ran away.

Colleen waited for a long time, but the kitten stayed hidden. So Colleen took the mother cat and the other kitten to safety.

Over the next few days, five other LICK rescuers went to the dumpster. They tried to find the kitten. They would hear her meow. They would even see her. But she was too quick to catch. So they left blankets to keep her warm.

The weather was getting worse. The radio warned of a big storm coming. It was a nor'easter. This type of storm can cause hurricane-force winds.

Peggy could only think about the poor little kitten. She was determined to rescue the kitten before the storm hit. So she packed her van with snacks and magazines. She was going to wait all night at the dumpster.

Peggy set the trap. Then she began the long wait. There was no kitten at 9 P.M. There was no kitten at 11 P.M., at midnight, or at 2 A.M.

Then the lights went out. Peggy was in complete darkness. Feeling a little scared, she drove to a nearby store that still had its lights on.

Once a kitten is ready to be adopted, the rescue group makes sure he is given a good home.

Rescue

She went back and forth to the trap. At 4 A.M., she looked again. The kitten was finally there!

It did not matter that it was so early. Peggy called Colleen right away. It was the best wake-up call Colleen could have gotten!

When she got home, Peggy placed the kitten with the kitten's mother and sister. The three of them snuggled together in soft, clean blankets.

The rescuers made sure the cats were healthy. They spayed them, to prevent them from having more unwanted kittens. Today, the cats are in good homes. They are clean, well fed, and loved.

"We are so glad to be able to give these cats a second chance," said Peggy. "Improving the life of homeless animals is the goal of all animal rescuers."

Chapter 2

History of the Cat

It is hard to imagine a world without cats. But that is how it was thousands of years ago. Back then people did not live in one spot. There were no houses or towns. People moved from place to place to find food.

As time passed, people learned to grow food. They stayed in one place. They built homes and towns.

That is when the rats came. The rats learned that they could get an easy meal. There were plenty of stored crops. Soon, towns were filled with rats, mice, and other pests.

The ancient Egyptians thought cats were very special. This is a bronze figure from Egypt after 600 B.C.E.

History of the Cat

Some scientists think that about twelve thousand years ago in the valley of the Nile, a river in Africa, something else happened. The African wildcats came from the forests. They came because they ate rats and mice and there were lots of them to eat in the towns.

The people did not want the rats and mice to eat their crops. So they started putting out fish heads and scraps for the wildcats. They wanted them to stay.

The wildcats had plenty of food. They were in a place safe from other animals that might eat them. People did not chase them away. So the African wildcats stayed. In time, they even allowed themselves to be petted and held. They became the ancestors of the cats we know today.

People have always liked cats. But the people of ancient Egypt really thought cats were special. The Egyptian leader, the pharaoh, said that cats were almost like gods. The Egyptians made sculptures and paintings of cats. They had laws against hurting cats. They made mummies of their cats to remember them forever when they died.

At first, cats only lived in Egypt, in the Nile Valley. They did not yet live in the rest of the world. Slowly, cats spread across the world. Ship captains kept cats on board to kill mice. Sometimes the cats had kittens. When the sailors came ashore, they gave the kittens away. As countries started trading more with each other, people took cats to these new places.

Today, cats are a familiar sight everywhere. Sometimes they still chase rats and mice like they did thousands of years ago. But mostly, cats are our special friends.

Chapter 3

Getting a Cat

Cats make great pets. They are loving, playful, and clean. Cats do not need a lot of space. They are happy living in a small apartment or a large house. Cats are good pets for people with busy lives.

Cats come in many different sizes and colors.

Getting a Cat

There are many different breeds of cats. The Cat Fanciers' Association lists forty kinds. These include the Siamese (sy-UH-meez), Persian (PER-shun), and Abyssinian (ab-UH-sin-ee-an), to name a few.

Each breed has its own characteristics. Siamese cats like lots of attention. They are known for being

Do you and your family want a mixed breed or purebred?

very talkative. Abyssinian cats have lots of energy and are known for making mischief. Persian cats are generally calmer. They enjoy sitting in your lap.

There are also mixed breed cats. They are sorted by the length of their fur. A domestic shorthair, or DSH, is any   short-haired mixed breed. A domestic longhair, or DLH, is   any long-haired mixed breed.

Cats also come in many different colors and coat patterns. For example, a striped coat of fur is called tabby. A white coat with patches of black and orange is known as calico. Whether you choose short hair or long, mixed breed or purebred, finding the right cat for your family is very important.

Knowing a little bit about the breed can help. All cats clean themselves, but they also enjoy being brushed by people. Long-haired cats require daily

Getting a Cat

brushing. This keeps their fur from getting matted, tangled, and stuck together. Short-haired cats do not need to be brushed as often.

Will you get a kitten or an adult cat? Kittens have lots of energy. They require more care and attention than adult cats. Sometimes kittens break things or knock things over when they are playing.

Kittens can be fun, but a lot of work!

Adult cats also like to play, but they are usually calmer. They do not need as much attention.

A great place to find your new cat is during an adoption day at a local pet store. Ask when a rescue group will be at the store.

You might consider adopting two cats. This way they can keep each other company. It is fun to watch them play together.

Find a cat with a personality that will fit your own personality and lifestyle. Some cats are shy. They may hide from you at first. It may take them a few days to trust you. Once they are no longer afraid, these shy cats will be sitting in your lap, purring and rubbing against you. Shy cats will sometimes form a strong bond with just one or two people. They may still get scared around strangers.

Other cats like everyone right away. They will jump into your lap. They are happy being with people.

Where will you get your cat? You can find many different types of cats at your local animal shelter. Shelters have kittens and adult cats, long-haired and short-haired, and even some purebreds.

Some cats are purebreds, like this Persian.

Getting a Cat

If you want a particular breed of cat that you cannot find at your local shelter, you may want to contact a breed rescue group. For example, a Siamese Rescue will have only Siamese cats. Many of the cats available at rescue groups are adult cats that have lost their homes.

The cost to adopt a cat from a shelter or rescue group is usually low. These places charge a fee to cover their costs in caring for the cats.

If you want a purebred cat—and if you are willing to spend more money—you can buy one from a breeder. Breeders raise cats of a certain type. You can usually meet the kitten's parents. That way you can know how the cat might turn out.

Some pet shops also sell kittens. Sometimes the animals at pet shops are treated well, but sometimes they are not.

Wherever you get her from, it is a good idea to have your new cat checked out by a veterinarian

When you first bring home your new pet, it is a good idea to take her to the vet. The vet will make sure your pet is healthy.

(vet). You can find one in your local yellow pages. You may also want to ask friends or neighbors for recommendations.

Make an appointment with your vet as soon as you can. A kitten will need several visits during his first year. Adult cats usually need just one visit each year, unless they get sick.

On the first visit, the vet will examine your cat. He will weigh her and take her temperature. The vet will look for fleas and worms. If vaccines are needed, he will give those shots.

The vet visit is also the time for you to ask questions. Write your questions down so you do not forget what you want to know.

Chapter 4
Health and Exercise

Get ready. You are going to bring your new cat home. Do you have a travel crate? A crate keeps your cat safe. Also, he will be less nervous in a crate.

Your cat will need a collar, food and water bowls, and a litter box. These are the basic supplies.

The collar should have an ID tag with your address and phone number.

Health and Exercise

A cat carrier is a safe way to carry your cat to the vet.

This way, if your cat gets lost, someone can return him to you. You may also want to microchip your cat. This means that a vet injects a microchip under the cat's skin. This type of ID is always with him. The tiny computer chip has a special code. If someone finds your cat, she can have him scanned by a veterinarian or an animal shelter. The microchip's special code will appear on the scanner and they will be able to find you.

24

Health and Exercise

Food and water bowls should be where the cat can easily find them. You can give him dry or wet food. Your vet can recommend a good brand of food and how much to feed your cat. You may decide to give your cat some human food too. Be careful. Human food might be dangerous for your pet. Check with your vet.

Place the food and water bowls where your cat can easily find them.

Health and Exercise

Cats are clean animals. They will look for a place to bury their waste. That is why it is not hard to teach a cat to do that in a litter box. Put the litter box in a spot that is easy for your cat to find but is not too busy or noisy. Keep the litter box clean. That means removing any waste each day and cleaning the whole box at least once a week.

Those are the supplies you need to start. But that is not the end of the list.

You might think your cat stays clean because he grooms himself. Cats lick their fur with long, sandpapery tongues. But they do need a little help.

You will need a special brush. This will help get rid of some of your cat's loose or matted hair. That means your cat will not swallow as much hair when he licks it. Short-haired cats do not need a lot of brushing. Long-haired cats need brushing every day.

Cats will clean themselves, but they still need to be brushed.

Healthy cats usually do not need baths. But if you do need to give your cat a bath, use a cat shampoo. Anything else can harm his skin.

You do not need a leash for your cat. Most cats do not enjoy being walked. In fact, cats should be kept indoors at all times. While you may know some

27

Make sure your cat has plenty of special cat toys!

outdoor cats, it is not safe to let your cat outside. Outdoor cats are in danger from cars, wild animals, diseases, and fleas.

It is good to socialize your cat. That means getting him used to people. Spend some time with your cat. Get him used to your voice. Some cats will always be shy around people. That is okay. The more time you spend with your cat, the more he will want to be with you.

You will find that your cat likes to play. You can get special toys at your local pet supply store. Do not let your cat play with string or yarn. He could accidentally swallow a piece and this will make him very sick.

You have given a loving home to a cat. Not all cats are so lucky. There are many homeless cats in the world. This problem is called pet overpopulation. That is why many people choose to spay or neuter their pets.

Health and Exercise

Spaying and neutering are operations that prevent animals from having babies. It is called spaying for a female and neutering for a male. Your veterinarian does these operations. Spaying or neutering your cat can make her or him healthier by preventing some types of diseases. Spaying or neutering will also prevent some bad behaviors, such as spraying urine. Also, cats that are spayed or neutered are not as likely to run away or get lost.

Usually, cats adopted from an animal shelter or breed rescue are already spayed or neutered. If you get a cat or kitten that has not been spayed or neutered, you should consider having this done. You will be helping to control pet overpopulation and will be giving your pet a healthier life.

Chapter 5

Problems and Challenges

Do you have a kitten? Young cats are very active. They like to explore everywhere. They can jump and reach places you may not want them to go to. Kittens also like to chew. It helps their mouths feel better when new teeth are coming in. If you have a kitten, you must "kitten proof" your home.

Take a look around. Is there anything breakable?

Problems and Challenges

Are there cords on the window shades that kittens can grab? Does your garbage have a cover? Is there anything sharp or dangerous within reach? Look carefully. Even some houseplants are poisonous to cats. Remove anything that could be unsafe.

Whether you have a kitten or an adult cat, you will want to know about hairballs. When cats groom themselves, they swallow hair. Hair is not easy to digest. It mixes with food in the stomach. Cats cough up the hair. Or hairballs might stay stuck inside. That hurts!

Regular brushing keeps cats from swallowing too much hair. But if your cat does swallow too much, you will want to

Cats can be very curious. Be sure to check your home for things that may be dangerous for your pet.

visit the vet. Watch your cat. Is he coughing a lot? Is he not eating or not using his litter box? That means something is wrong.

See the vet, too, if your cat has fleas. You might see them on her skin. Or you might see her scratching. Fleas are itchy and uncomfortable. Cats can catch diseases from them. Fleas can also bite people, like you and your family.

Your vet can treat your cat if he has fleas. She can also give you medicine that prevents fleas.

Fleas, hairballs, and kitten proofing are common challenges. Here are some other situations you might come across.

other Animals

Do you have another cat or dog? You will have to introduce your new cat carefully. Start by letting them sniff each other through a gate. Then hold one animal and let the other sniff. Reverse the situation.

Do this for several days. Slowly increase the time the animals spend together. Do not leave them alone until you know that they have become used to each other.

Be patient. Sometimes, your new cat and other pets will accept each other right away, but sometimes it can take a few weeks or even a few months.

Clawing Furniture and Carpets

Cats like to scratch. It helps keep their claws sharp. But this habit can damage your furniture or carpeting.

You will need to buy a scratching post so that your cat will learn to use this instead of your furniture or rugs. There are several different kinds. Some are

If your cat is acting strangely or looks sick, take him to the vet right away.

made of carpet or cardboard. Others are made of sisal, a stiff material that is like a rope.

Some scratching posts stand straight up. Others lie flat. Most cats will prefer one kind. You may need to try different kinds to find out which your cat likes best. You can attract your cat to his scratching post by sprinkling some catnip on it.

To stop a cat from scratching your sofa, you can use special sticky tape on the back or sides. Cats do

Your vet can show you how to clip your cat's nails.

not like the feel of this tape. They will quickly find a new favorite scratching place. That is the perfect time for them to start using a scratching post.

You can also buy soft caps to put over a cat's claws. That way, when he scratches, he will not cause any damage. These caps are safe for your cat and even come in different colors. They need to be replaced about once a month.

You may want to learn to trim your cat's nails. Keeping the claws short will help save your furniture. It will also prevent you from getting scratched accidentally when you hold your cat. Your veterinarian can show you how to trim your cat's nails safely.

Some people choose to remove their cat's claws. This operation is known as declawing. This is not a good idea. It is a painful healing process after the operation. But that is not all. A declawed cat will not be able to defend herself. She cannot climb to escape danger should she accidentally get outside. Declawing can actually change a cat's personality. She may become aggressive, and bite and hiss. Or she may avoid people or animals, feeling as if she cannot protect herself.

Spraying and Accidents

Cats who are not spayed or neutered will sometimes spray urine on walls and furniture. They do this to mark their territory. You can usually prevent this behavior by having your cat spayed or neutered. But sometimes neutered cats will also spray urine. They may do this when they feel stressed or upset by something. A move to a new house or a new cat or dog can be a cause. Peeing outside the litter box may also be a sign that your cat is sick. Check with your veterinarian to help you find the cause of this behavior and get the right treatment.

38

Problems and Challenges

With a little bit of patience, every member of your family will welcome your new cat—even the dog!

curtain climbing

Cats like to climb, and curtains can be irresistible—especially for kittens. Make sure that you open your curtains during the day so that your cat can look out the window. Some cats may be climbing just to try to get a look outside.

If you see your cat on the curtain, you can squirt a water bottle at her and say, 'no.' A sudden noise, such as clapping your hands, can also work. When you cannot be there, try switching the curtain to a tension rod. This will cause the rod and curtain to fall down every time she climbs. That is just no fun.

You can always replace your curtains with blinds. Cats do not usually climb those.

Biting

Kittens play by using their sharp little teeth. But they need to learn that they cannot play that way with people.

When your kitten nips you in play, let him know it hurts. Make a loud squeal. Leave the kitten alone. Do not give him any attention. Then, after a few minutes, try again. The kitten will learn that biting causes the play to stop.

If your adult cat bites, that is a more serious problem. Biting, hissing, and growling are signs of aggression. You want to be careful in dealing with cats like this. Talk to your vet about what you can do to keep you and your cat safe.

Chapter 6
A Lifelong Responsibility

The cat you bring home will probably share your life for fifteen to twenty years. In return for food, shelter, and medical care, she will give you so much in return.

Cats can improve our moods!

A Lifelong Responsibility

Cats can keep us from feeling lonely. They are always there to happily greet us. They snuggle with us and purr and entertain us when they play. Cats can even be good listeners. In these ways, they reduce stress. They help to make us happier people.

Millions of people own cats. Celebrities now and throughout history have formed close relationships with them.

Sir Winston Churchill, the prime minister of England during World War II, had a cat named Jock. The cat used to go to meetings with his owner. The two would also eat dinner together. If Jock was late to dinner, Sir Winston sent his servants to find him. He would not eat until the cat was there.

Author Mark Twain had eleven cats. They lived on his farm in Connecticut. He wrote, "I simply can't resist a cat, particularly a purring one."

President Bill Clinton and his family owned a

Taking good care of your pet will bring you years of happiness.

black-and-white domestic shorthair named Socks. Socks lived in the White House during the eight years Clinton was president.

Today's stars love cats, too. Zac Efron has a Siamese cat named Simon. Cameron Diaz has a cat named Little Man.

You do not have to be famous or live in the White House to give a cat a good home. Simply take the time to care for your pet. Make a difference in his life and you will have a friend for many years.

aggression—Biting, growling, hissing, or other behavior that indicates your cat may attack.

animal shelter—An organization that cares for homeless pets.

breed—A type of cat that came from a common ancestor.

fleas—Small, wingless insects that feed on blood.

hairball—A clump of hair that can get stuck with food in a cat's digestive system.

microchip—A computer chip ID that is injected under the skin of your cat, usually between the shoulder blades.

neutering—An operation on a male cat to prevent babies.

rescue group—A group that finds homes for needy and unwanted animals.

spaying—An operation on a female cat to prevent babies.

vaccines—Shots to prevent disease.

veterinarian ("vet")—A doctor specializing in animals.

Further Reading

Books

Alderton, David. *Cats*. New York: DK
    Publishing, 2003.

Blackaby, Susan. *A Cat for You: Caring for Your Cat*.
    Mankato, Minn.: Picture Window
    Books, 2003.

Landau, Elaine. *Your Pet Cat*. New York:
    Children's Press, 2007.

Miller, Sara Swan. *Three More Stories You Can Read
    to Your Cat*. Boston: Houghton Mifflin, 2002.

Strachan, Jackie. *50 Games to Play With Your Cat*.
    Neptune, N.J.: TFH Publications, 2007.

Further Reading

Internet Addresses

American Humane Association
    <http://www.americanhumane.org>

Animal Planet—Pets
    <http://animal.discovery.com/petplanet/>

LICK, Life Improvement for Cats and Kittens
    <http://www.catsandkittens.org>